MY PLANNER

for success

This planner belongs to:

Copyright © 2021 Boss Branding on a Budget LLC
all rights reserved.

No parts of this book may be reproduced, distributed, or transmitted in any form without written permission from the publisher.

For more information about business marketing and social media management please visit www.BossBrandingonaBudget.com

Thank you so much for purchasing this planner. Your purchase helps a small business, and if this planner is used property, you have the potential to advance your business.

My goal is to provide solutions to help small business owners like yourself succeed.

Now start planning your yearly, quarterly, monthly, weekly business goals!

Don't forget to tag us on social media!

@BossBrandingonaBudget

PLANNING
and
Scheduling

I AM SURROUNDED BY ABUNDANCE EVERY DAY.

JANUARY

MONDAY	TUESDAY	WEDNESDAY	THURSDAY	FRIDAY	SATURDAY	SUNDAY
☐	☐	☐	☐	☐	☐	☐
☐	☐	☐	☐	☐	☐	☐
☐	☐	☐	☐	☐	☐	☐
☐	☐	☐	☐	☐	☐	☐
☐	☐	☐	☐	☐	☐	☐
☐	☐	☐	☐	☐	☐	☐

30-DAY *productivity challenge*

30-days to becoming more productive!

Create a master to-do list	Take a 24 hour tv break	Take a break from social media	Do some goal planning	Work towards 1 goal today
Do 20 minutes of exercise	Clean your bedroom cupboards	Clean your kitchen cupboards	Wake up earlier	Reduce any distractions
Meet a new milestone	Organize your desktop	Plan your days in advance	Do meal planning	Create a productivity music playlist
Check your emails regularly	Do the most important thing first	Delegate an unimportant task	Make use of planning tools	Stop multitasking
Take short breaks between tasks	Get 8 hours of sleep	Drink enough water	Batch smaller tasks	Find your peak productivity time
Learn to say no	Set boundaries	Be realistic about your goals	Be intentional with your thoughts	Work smarter

You got this!

MONTHLY *planner*

Month: **Main focus:**

Week 1 Week 2 To-do list

Week 1 Week 2

Notes

WEEKLY *planner*

Week: **Quote:**

Monday

Tuesday

Wednesday

Thursday

Friday

Saturday

Sunday

WEEKLY planner

Week: **Quote:**

Monday

Tuesday

Wednesday

Thursday

Friday

Saturday

Sunday

WEEKLY *planner*

Week: **Quote:**

Monday

Tuesday

Wednesday

Thursday

Friday

Saturday

Sunday

WEEKLY

Week: **Quote:**

Monday

Tuesday

Wednesday

Thursday

Friday

Saturday

Sunday

Date -

Main focus -

Start date -

End date -

Breakdown of main focus

Smaller tasks to accomplish

- [ ] _____
- [ ] _____
- [ ] _____
- [ ] _____
- [ ] _____
- [ ] _____
- [ ] _____
- [ ] _____
- [ ] _____
- [ ] _____
- [ ] _____

Notes

PROJECT

Start date

End date

Objective of project

MILESTONES

_____
_____
_____
_____

Task	Assigned to	Done

notes

TO-DO *list*

Date -

HIGH PRIORITY   LOW PRIORITY

○ _____   ○ _____
○ _____   ○ _____
○ _____   ○ _____
○ _____   ○ _____
○ _____   ○ _____
○ _____   ○ _____
○ _____   ○ _____
○ _____   ○ _____
○ _____   ○ _____
○ _____   ○ _____

Notes

_____
_____
_____

THINGS I *need to do*

Month - _____

Week _____

MONDAY
- [ ] _____
- [ ] _____
- [ ] _____
- [ ] _____
- [ ] _____

TUESDAY
- [ ] _____
- [ ] _____
- [ ] _____
- [ ] _____
- [ ] _____

WEDNESDAY
- [ ] _____
- [ ] _____
- [ ] _____
- [ ] _____
- [ ] _____

THURSDAY
- [ ] _____
- [ ] _____
- [ ] _____
- [ ] _____
- [ ] _____

FRIDAY
- [ ] _____
- [ ] _____
- [ ] _____
- [ ] _____
- [ ] _____

SATURDAY
- [ ] _____
- [ ] _____
- [ ] _____
- [ ] _____
- [ ] _____

SUNDAY
- [ ] _____
- [ ] _____
- [ ] _____
- [ ] _____
- [ ] _____

IMPORTANT NOTES
_____
_____
_____
_____
_____

MEETING *notes*

Meeting name/topic	Time	Date

Attendess

_____   _____
_____   _____
_____   _____
_____   _____

Agenda

_____
_____
_____
_____
_____
_____
_____
_____

objectives

PRIORITY

INSTRUCTIONS
List all the tasks you need to get done in the priority matrix below. Start with the most important and most urgent. The priority matrix will help you determine what needs to get done now and how you can better balance all the tasks that you need to do

	DO NOW	DO LATER
IMPORTANT	**GET IT DONE** (Important & urgent)	**SCHEDULE IT** (Important - not urgent)
NOT IMPORTANT	**DELEGATE IT** (Who else can do it)	**ELIMINATE IT** (not important, not urgent - delete)

BUCKET *list*

○ _____ ○ _____

○ _____ ○ _____

○ _____ ○ _____

○ _____ ○ _____

○ _____ ○ _____

○ _____ ○ _____

○ _____ ○ _____

○ _____ ○ _____

○ _____ ○ _____

○ _____ ○ _____

○ _____ ○ _____

○ _____ ○ _____

○ _____ ○ _____

○ _____ ○ _____

○ _____ ○ _____

I AM IN THE PROCESS OF BECOMING THE BEST VERSION OF MYSELF.

FEBRUARY

MONDAY	TUESDAY	WEDNESDAY	THURSDAY	FRIDAY	SATURDAY	SUNDAY
☐	☐	☐	☐	☐	☐	☐
☐	☐	☐	☐	☐	☐	☐
☐	☐	☐	☐	☐	☐	☐
☐	☐	☐	☐	☐	☐	☐
☐	☐	☐	☐	☐	☐	☐
☐	☐	☐	☐	☐	☐	☐

30-DAY *productivity challenge*

30-days to becoming more productive!

Create a master to-do list	Take a 24 hour tv break	Take a break from social media	Do some goal planning	Work towards 1 goal today
Do 20 minutes of exercise	Clean your bedroom cupboards	Clean your kitchen cupboards	Wake up earlier	Reduce any distractions
Meet a new milestone	Organize your desktop	Plan your days in advance	Do meal planning	Create a productivity music playlist
Check your emails regularly	Do the most important thing first	Delegate an unimportant task	Make use of planning tools	Stop multitasking
Take short breaks between tasks	Get 8 hours of sleep	Drink enough water	Batch smaller tasks	Find your peak productivity time
Learn to say no	Set boundaries	Be realistic about your goals	Be intentional with your thoughts	Work smarter

You got this!

MONTHLY *planner*

Month: **Main focus:**

| Week 1 | Week 2 |

To-do list

- _____ ☐
- _____ ☐
- _____ ☐
- _____ ☐
- _____ ☐
- _____ ☐
- _____ ☐
- _____ ☐
- _____ ☐
- _____ ☐
- _____ ☐
- _____ ☐
- _____ ☐
- _____ ☐

| Week 1 | Week 2 |

Notes

WEEKLY planner

Week: **Quote:**

Monday

Tuesday

Wednesday

Thursday

Friday

Saturday

Sunday

Week: **Quote:**

Monday

Tuesday

Wednesday

Thursday

Friday

Saturday

Sunday

WEEKLY planner

Week: **Quote:**

Monday

Tuesday

Wednesday

Thursday

Friday

Saturday

Sunday

WEEKLY *planner*

Week: **Quote:**

Monday

Tuesday

Wednesday

Thursday

Friday

Saturday

Sunday

Date -

Main focus -

Start date -

End date -

Breakdown of main focus

Smaller tasks to accomplish

- [ ]
- [ ]
- [ ]
- [ ]
- [ ]
- [ ]
- [ ]
- [ ]
- [ ]
- [ ]
- [ ]
- [ ]

Notes

Start date

End date

Objective of project

MILESTONES

Task	Assigned to	Done

notes

TO-DO List

Date -

HIGH PRIORITY

- _____
- _____
- _____
- _____
- _____
- _____
- _____
- _____
- _____
- _____

LOW PRIORITY

- _____
- _____
- _____
- _____
- _____
- _____
- _____
- _____
- _____
- _____

THINGS I *need to do*

Month - _____

Week _____

MONDAY
- [ ] _____
- [ ] _____
- [ ] _____
- [ ] _____
- [ ] _____

TUESDAY
- [ ] _____
- [ ] _____
- [ ] _____
- [ ] _____
- [ ] _____

WEDNESDAY
- [ ] _____
- [ ] _____
- [ ] _____
- [ ] _____
- [ ] _____

THURSDAY
- [ ] _____
- [ ] _____
- [ ] _____
- [ ] _____
- [ ] _____

FRIDAY
- [ ] _____
- [ ] _____
- [ ] _____
- [ ] _____
- [ ] _____

SATURDAY
- [ ] _____
- [ ] _____
- [ ] _____
- [ ] _____
- [ ] _____

SUNDAY
- [ ] _____
- [ ] _____
- [ ] _____
- [ ] _____
- [ ] _____

IMPORTANT NOTES
_____
_____
_____
_____
_____

MEETING *notes*

Meeting name/topic	Time	Date

Attendess

_____   _____

_____   _____

_____   _____

_____   _____

Agenda

_____

_____

_____

_____

_____

_____

_____

objectives

PRIORITY

INSTRUCTIONS
List all the tasks you need to get done in the priority matrix below. Start with the most important and most urgent. The priority matrix will help you determine what needs to get done now and how you can better balance all the tasks that you need to do

	DO NOW	DO LATER
IMPORTANT	**GET IT DONE** (Important & urgent)	**SCHEDULE IT** (Important - not urgent)
NOT IMPORTANT	**DELEGATE IT** (Who else can do it)	**ELIMINATE IT** (not important, not urgent - delete)

BUCKET *list*

- ○ _____
- ○ _____
- ○ _____
- ○ _____
- ○ _____
- ○ _____
- ○ _____
- ○ _____
- ○ _____
- ○ _____
- ○ _____
- ○ _____
- ○ _____
- ○ _____

- ○ _____
- ○ _____
- ○ _____
- ○ _____
- ○ _____
- ○ _____
- ○ _____
- ○ _____
- ○ _____
- ○ _____
- ○ _____
- ○ _____
- ○ _____
- ○ _____

I ALREADY HAVE EVERYTHING I NEED TO CREATE SUCCESS IN MY BUSINESS.

MARCH

MONDAY	TUESDAY	WEDNESDAY	THURSDAY	FRIDAY	SATURDAY	SUNDAY
☐	☐	☐	☐	☐	☐	☐
☐	☐	☐	☐	☐	☐	☐
☐	☐	☐	☐	☐	☐	☐
☐	☐	☐	☐	☐	☐	☐
☐	☐	☐	☐	☐	☐	☐
☐	☐	☐	☐	☐	☐	☐

30-DAY *productivity challenge*

30-days to becoming more productive!

Create a master to-do list	Take a 24 hour tv break	Take a break from social media	Do some goal planning	Work towards 1 goal today
Do 20 minutes of exercise	Clean your bedroom cupboards	Clean your kitchen cupboards	Wake up earlier	Reduce any distractions
Meet a new milestone	Organize your desktop	Plan your days in advance	Do meal planning	Create a productivity music playlist
Check your emails regularly	Do the most important thing first	Delegate an unimportant task	Make use of planning tools	Stop multitasking
Take short breaks between tasks	Get 8 hours of sleep	Drink enough water	Batch smaller tasks	Find your peak productivity time
Learn to say no	Set boundaries	Be realistic about your goals	Be intentional with your thoughts	Work smarter

You got this!

MONTHLY *planner*

Month: **Main focus:**

Week 1   Week 2   To-do list

Week 1   Week 2

Notes

WEEKLY *planner*

Week: **Quote:**

Monday

Tuesday

Wednesday

Thursday

Friday

Saturday

Sunday

WEEKLY *planner*

Week: **Quote:**

Monday

Tuesday

Wednesday

Thursday

Friday

Saturday

Sunday

WEEKLY *planner*

Week: **Quote:**

Monday

Tuesday

Wednesday

Thursday

Friday

Saturday

Sunday

WEEKLY *planner*

Week: **Quote:**

Monday

Tuesday

Wednesday

Thursday

Friday

Saturday

Sunday

FOCUS *planner*

Date -

Main focus -

Start date -

End date -

Breakdown of main focus

Smaller tasks to accomplish

☐
☐
☐
☐
☐
☐
☐
☐
☐
☐
☐

Notes

PROJECT *planner*

Start date

End date

Objective of project

MILESTONES

Task	Assigned to	Done

notes

TO-DO *list*

Date -

HIGH PRIORITY	LOW PRIORITY
○ _____	○ _____
○ _____	○ _____
○ _____	○ _____
○ _____	○ _____
○ _____	○ _____
○ _____	○ _____
○ _____	○ _____
○ _____	○ _____
○ _____	○ _____
○ _____	○ _____

Notes

_____
_____
_____

THINGS I *need to do*

Month - _____

Week _____

MONDAY
- [ ] _____
- [ ] _____
- [ ] _____
- [ ] _____
- [ ] _____

TUESDAY
- [ ] _____
- [ ] _____
- [ ] _____
- [ ] _____
- [ ] _____

WEDNESDAY
- [ ] _____
- [ ] _____
- [ ] _____
- [ ] _____
- [ ] _____

THURSDAY
- [ ] _____
- [ ] _____
- [ ] _____
- [ ] _____
- [ ] _____

FRIDAY
- [ ] _____
- [ ] _____
- [ ] _____
- [ ] _____
- [ ] _____

SATURDAY
- [ ] _____
- [ ] _____
- [ ] _____
- [ ] _____
- [ ] _____

SUNDAY
- [ ] _____
- [ ] _____
- [ ] _____
- [ ] _____
- [ ] _____

IMPORTANT NOTES
_____
_____
_____
_____
_____

MEETING *notes*

Meeting name/topic	Time	Date

Attendess

_____   _____
_____   _____
_____   _____
_____   _____

Agenda

_____
_____
_____
_____
_____
_____
_____

objectives

PRIORITY *matrix*

INSTRUCTIONS
List all the tasks you need to get done in the priority matrix below. Start with the most important and most urgent. The priority matrix will help you determine what needs to get done now and how you can better balance all the tasks that you need to do

	DO NOW	DO LATER
IMPORTANT	**GET IT DONE** (Important & urgent)	**SCHEDULE IT** (Important - not urgent)
NOT IMPORTANT	**DELEGATE IT** (Who else can do it)	**ELIMINATE IT** (not important, not urgent - delete)

BUCKET *list*

○ _____
○ _____
○ _____
○ _____
○ _____
○ _____
○ _____
○ _____
○ _____
○ _____
○ _____
○ _____
○ _____
○ _____
○ _____

○ _____
○ _____
○ _____
○ _____
○ _____
○ _____
○ _____
○ _____
○ _____
○ _____
○ _____
○ _____
○ _____
○ _____
○ _____

I AM EXACTLY WHERE I AM MEANT TO BE.

APRIL

MONDAY	TUESDAY	WEDNESDAY	THURSDAY	FRIDAY	SATURDAY	SUNDAY
☐	☐	☐	☐	☐	☐	☐
☐	☐	☐	☐	☐	☐	☐
☐	☐	☐	☐	☐	☐	☐
☐	☐	☐	☐	☐	☐	☐
☐	☐	☐	☐	☐	☐	☐
☐	☐	☐	☐	☐	☐	☐

30-DAY *productivity challenge*

30-days to becoming more productive!

Create a master to-do list	Take a 24 hour tv break	Take a break from social media	Do some goal planning	Work towards 1 goal today
Do 20 minutes of exercise	Clean your bedroom cupboards	Clean your kitchen cupboards	Wake up earlier	Reduce any distractions
Meet a new milestone	Organize your desktop	Plan your days in advance	Do meal planning	Create a productivity music playlist
Check your emails regularly	Do the most important thing first	Delegate an unimportant task	Make use of planning tools	Stop multitasking
Take short breaks between tasks	Get 8 hours of sleep	Drink enough water	Batch smaller tasks	Find your peak productivity time
Learn to say no	Set boundaries	Be realistic about your goals	Be intentional with your thoughts	Work *smarter*

You got this!

MONTHLY *planner*

Month: **Main focus:**

Week 1	Week 2	To-do list
		☐
		☐
		☐
		☐
		☐
		☐
		☐

Week 1	Week 2	
		☐
		☐
		☐
		☐
		☐
		☐
		☐

Notes

WEEKLY *planner*

Week: **Quote:**

Monday

Tuesday

Wednesday

Thursday

Friday

Saturday

Sunday

WEEKLY *planner*

Week: **Quote:**

Monday

Tuesday

Wednesday

Thursday

Friday

Saturday

Sunday

WEEKLY *planner*

Week: **Quote:**

Monday

Tuesday

Wednesday

Thursday

Friday

Saturday

Sunday

WEEKLY *planner*

Week: **Quote:**

Monday

Tuesday

Wednesday

Thursday

Friday

Saturday

Sunday

FOCUS *planner*

Date -

Main focus -

Start date -

End date -

Breakdown of main focus

Smaller tasks to accomplish

- [ ]
- [ ]
- [ ]
- [ ]
- [ ]
- [ ]
- [ ]
- [ ]
- [ ]
- [ ]
- [ ]

Notes

PROJECT *planner*

Start date

End date

Objective of project

MILESTONES

Task	Assigned to	Done

notes

TO-DO *list*

Date -

HIGH PRIORITY | LOW PRIORITY

○ _____   ○ _____
○ _____   ○ _____
○ _____   ○ _____
○ _____   ○ _____
○ _____   ○ _____
○ _____   ○ _____
○ _____   ○ _____
○ _____   ○ _____
○ _____   ○ _____
○ _____   ○ _____

Notes

_____
_____
_____

THINGS I *need to do*

Month - _____

Week _____

MONDAY
- [ ] _____
- [ ] _____
- [ ] _____
- [ ] _____
- [ ] _____

TUESDAY
- [ ] _____
- [ ] _____
- [ ] _____
- [ ] _____
- [ ] _____

WEDNESDAY
- [ ] _____
- [ ] _____
- [ ] _____
- [ ] _____
- [ ] _____

THURSDAY
- [ ] _____
- [ ] _____
- [ ] _____
- [ ] _____
- [ ] _____

FRIDAY
- [ ] _____
- [ ] _____
- [ ] _____
- [ ] _____
- [ ] _____

SATURDAY
- [ ] _____
- [ ] _____
- [ ] _____
- [ ] _____
- [ ] _____

SUNDAY
- [ ] _____
- [ ] _____
- [ ] _____
- [ ] _____
- [ ] _____

IMPORTANT NOTES
_____
_____
_____
_____
_____

MEETING *notes*

Meeting name/topic	Time	Date

Attendess

Agenda

objectives

PRIORITY *matrix*

INSTRUCTIONS
List all the tasks you need to get done in the priority matrix below. Start with the most important and most urgent. The priority matrix will help you determine what needs to get done now and how you can better balance all the tasks that you need to do

	DO NOW	DO LATER
IMPORTANT	**GET IT DONE** (Important & urgent)	**SCHEDULE IT** (Important - not urgent)
NOT IMPORTANT	**DELEGATE IT** (Who else can do it)	**ELIMINATE IT** (not important, not urgent - delete)

BUCKET *list*

○ _____ ○ _____
○ _____ ○ _____
○ _____ ○ _____
○ _____ ○ _____
○ _____ ○ _____
○ _____ ○ _____
○ _____ ○ _____
○ _____ ○ _____
○ _____ ○ _____
○ _____ ○ _____
○ _____ ○ _____
○ _____ ○ _____
○ _____ ○ _____
○ _____ ○ _____

I HANDLE SUCCESS WITH GRATITUDE AND GRACE.

MAY

MONDAY	TUESDAY	WEDNESDAY	THURSDAY	FRIDAY	SATURDAY	SUNDAY
☐	☐	☐	☐	☐	☐	☐
☐	☐	☐	☐	☐	☐	☐
☐	☐	☐	☐	☐	☐	☐
☐	☐	☐	☐	☐	☐	☐
☐	☐	☐	☐	☐	☐	☐
☐	☐	☐	☐	☐	☐	☐

30-DAY *productivity challenge*

30-days to becoming more productive!

Create a master to-do list	Take a 24 hour tv break	Take a break from social media	Do some goal planning	Work towards 1 goal today
Do 20 minutes of exercise	Clean your bedroom cupboards	Clean your kitchen cupboards	Wake up earlier	Reduce any distractions
Meet a new milestone	Organize your desktop	Plan your days in advance	Do meal planning	Create a productivity music playlist
Check your emails regularly	Do the most important thing first	Delegate an unimportant task	Make use of planning tools	Stop multitasking
Take short breaks between tasks	Get 8 hours of sleep	Drink enough water	Batch smaller tasks	Find your peak productivity time
Learn to say no	Set boundaries	Be realistic about your goals	Be intentional with your thoughts	Work smarter

You got this!

MONTHLY *planner*

Month: **Main focus:**

| Week 1 | Week 2 | To-do list |

☐
☐
☐
☐
☐
☐
☐
☐
☐
☐
☐
☐
☐
☐

| Week 1 | Week 2 |

Notes

WEEKLY *planner*

Week: **Quote:**

Monday

Tuesday

Wednesday

Thursday

Friday

Saturday

Sunday

WEEKLY *planner*

Week: **Quote:**

Monday

Tuesday

Wednesday

Thursday

Friday

Saturday

Sunday

WEEKLY *planner*

Week: **Quote:**

Monday

Tuesday

Wednesday

Thursday

Friday

Saturday

Sunday

WEEKLY *planner*

Week: **Quote:**

Monday

Tuesday

Wednesday

Thursday

Friday

Saturday

Sunday

FOCUS *planner*

Date -

Main focus -

Start date -

End date -

Breakdown of main focus

Smaller tasks to accomplish

- [ ]
- [ ]
- [ ]
- [ ]
- [ ]
- [ ]
- [ ]
- [ ]
- [ ]
- [ ]
- [ ]

Notes

PROJECT *planner*

Start date

End date

Objective of project

MILESTONES

Task	Assigned to	Done

notes

TO-DO *list*

Date -

HIGH PRIORITY

- ○ _____
- ○ _____
- ○ _____
- ○ _____
- ○ _____
- ○ _____
- ○ _____
- ○ _____
- ○ _____
- ○ _____

LOW PRIORITY

- ○ _____
- ○ _____
- ○ _____
- ○ _____
- ○ _____
- ○ _____
- ○ _____
- ○ _____
- ○ _____
- ○ _____

Notes

_____
_____
_____

THINGS I *need to do*

Month - _____

Week _____

" "

MONDAY
- [ ] _____
- [ ] _____
- [ ] _____
- [ ] _____
- [ ] _____

TUESDAY
- [ ] _____
- [ ] _____
- [ ] _____
- [ ] _____
- [ ] _____

WEDNESDAY
- [ ] _____
- [ ] _____
- [ ] _____
- [ ] _____
- [ ] _____

THURSDAY
- [ ] _____
- [ ] _____
- [ ] _____
- [ ] _____
- [ ] _____

FRIDAY
- [ ] _____
- [ ] _____
- [ ] _____
- [ ] _____
- [ ] _____

SATURDAY
- [ ] _____
- [ ] _____
- [ ] _____
- [ ] _____
- [ ] _____

SUNDAY
- [ ] _____
- [ ] _____
- [ ] _____
- [ ] _____
- [ ] _____

IMPORTANT NOTES
_____
_____
_____
_____
_____

MEETING *notes*

Meeting name/topic	Time	Date

Attendess

_____   _____

_____   _____

_____   _____

_____   _____

Agenda

_____

_____

_____

_____

_____

_____

_____

objectives

PRIORITY *matrix*

INSTRUCTIONS
List all the tasks you need to get done in the priority matrix below. Start with the most important and most urgent. The priority matrix will help you determine what needs to get done now and how you can better balance all the tasks that you need to do

	DO NOW	DO LATER
IMPORTANT	**GET IT DONE** (Important & urgent)	**SCHEDULE IT** (Important - not urgent)
NOT IMPORTANT	**DELEGATE IT** (Who else can do it)	**ELIMINATE IT** (not important, not urgent - delete)

BUCKET *list*

- ○ _____
- ○ _____
- ○ _____
- ○ _____
- ○ _____
- ○ _____
- ○ _____
- ○ _____
- ○ _____
- ○ _____
- ○ _____
- ○ _____
- ○ _____
- ○ _____

- ○ _____
- ○ _____
- ○ _____
- ○ _____
- ○ _____
- ○ _____
- ○ _____
- ○ _____
- ○ _____
- ○ _____
- ○ _____
- ○ _____
- ○ _____
- ○ _____

I HAVE FAITH IN MYSELF AND IN MY ABILITIES.

JUNE

MONDAY	TUESDAY	WEDNESDAY	THURSDAY	FRIDAY	SATURDAY	SUNDAY
☐	☐	☐	☐	☐	☐	☐
☐	☐	☐	☐	☐	☐	☐
☐	☐	☐	☐	☐	☐	☐
☐	☐	☐	☐	☐	☐	☐
☐	☐	☐	☐	☐	☐	☐
☐	☐	☐	☐	☐	☐	☐

30-DAY *productivity challenge*

30-days to becoming more productive!

Create a master to-do list	Take a 24 hour tv break	Take a break from social media	Do some goal planning	Work towards 1 goal today
Do 20 minutes of exercise	Clean your bedroom cupboards	Clean your kitchen cupboards	Wake up earlier	Reduce any distractions
Meet a new milestone	Organize your desktop	Plan your days in advance	Do meal planning	Create a productivity music playlist
Check your emails regularly	Do the most important thing first	Delegate an unimportant task	Make use of planning tools	Stop multitasking
Take short breaks between tasks	Get 8 hours of sleep	Drink enough water	Batch smaller tasks	Find your peak productivity time
Learn to say no	Set boundaries	Be realistic about your goals	Be intentional with your thoughts	Work smarter

You got this!

MONTHLY *planner*

Month: **Main focus:**

Week 1

Week 2

Week 1

Week 2

To-do list

_____ ☐
_____ ☐
_____ ☐
_____ ☐
_____ ☐
_____ ☐
_____ ☐
_____ ☐
_____ ☐
_____ ☐
_____ ☐
_____ ☐
_____ ☐
_____ ☐

Notes

WEEKLY *planner*

Week: **Quote:**

Monday

Tuesday

Wednesday

Thursday

Friday

Saturday

Sunday

WEEKLY *planner*

Week: **Quote:**

Monday

Tuesday

Wednesday

Thursday

Friday

Saturday

Sunday

WEEKLY *planner*

Week: **Quote:**

Monday

Tuesday

Wednesday

Thursday

Friday

Saturday

Sunday

WEEKLY *planner*

Week: **Quote:**

Monday

Tuesday

Wednesday

Thursday

Friday

Saturday

Sunday

FOCUS *planner*

Date -
Main focus -

Start date -
End date -

Breakdown of main focus

Smaller tasks to accomplish

- [ ]
- [ ]
- [ ]
- [ ]
- [ ]
- [ ]
- [ ]
- [ ]
- [ ]
- [ ]
- [ ]

Notes

PROJECT *planner*

Start date

End date

Objective of project

MILESTONES

_____
_____
_____
_____

Task   Assigned to   Done

notes

TO-DO *list*

Date -

HIGH PRIORITY — LOW PRIORITY

○ _____ ○ _____
○ _____ ○ _____
○ _____ ○ _____
○ _____ ○ _____
○ _____ ○ _____
○ _____ ○ _____
○ _____ ○ _____
○ _____ ○ _____
○ _____ ○ _____
○ _____ ○ _____

THINGS I *need to do*

Month - _____

Week _____

MONDAY
- [ ] _____
- [ ] _____
- [ ] _____
- [ ] _____
- [ ] _____

TUESDAY
- [ ] _____
- [ ] _____
- [ ] _____
- [ ] _____
- [ ] _____

WEDNESDAY
- [ ] _____
- [ ] _____
- [ ] _____
- [ ] _____
- [ ] _____

THURSDAY
- [ ] _____
- [ ] _____
- [ ] _____
- [ ] _____
- [ ] _____

FRIDAY
- [ ] _____
- [ ] _____
- [ ] _____
- [ ] _____
- [ ] _____

SATURDAY
- [ ] _____
- [ ] _____
- [ ] _____
- [ ] _____
- [ ] _____

SUNDAY
- [ ] _____
- [ ] _____
- [ ] _____
- [ ] _____
- [ ] _____

IMPORTANT NOTES
_____
_____
_____
_____
_____

MEETING *notes*

Meeting name/topic	Time	Date

Attendess

Agenda

objectives

PRIORITY *matrix*

INSTRUCTIONS
List all the tasks you need to get done in the priority matrix below. Start with the most important and most urgent. The priority matrix will help you determine what needs to get done now and how you can better balance all the tasks that you need to do

	DO NOW	DO LATER
IMPORTANT	**GET IT DONE** (Important & urgent)	**SCHEDULE IT** (Important - not urgent)
NOT IMPORTANT	**DELEGATE IT** (Who else can do it)	**ELIMINATE IT** (not important, not urgent - delete)

BUCKET *list*

SUCCESS IS ENJOYING LIFE – I CAN DO THAT NOW!

JULY

MONDAY	TUESDAY	WEDNESDAY	THURSDAY	FRIDAY	SATURDAY	SUNDAY
☐	☐	☐	☐	☐	☐	☐
☐	☐	☐	☐	☐	☐	☐
☐	☐	☐	☐	☐	☐	☐
☐	☐	☐	☐	☐	☐	☐
☐	☐	☐	☐	☐	☐	☐
☐	☐	☐	☐	☐	☐	☐

30-DAY *productivity challenge*

30-days to becoming more productive!

Create a master to-do list	Take a 24 hour tv break	Take a break from social media	Do some goal planning	Work towards 1 goal today
Do 20 minutes of exercise	Clean your bedroom cupboards	Clean your kitchen cupboards	Wake up earlier	Reduce any distractions
Meet a new milestone	Organize your desktop	Plan your days in advance	Do meal planning	Create a productivity music playlist
Check your emails regularly	Do the most important thing first	Delegate an unimportant task	Make use of planning tools	Stop multitasking
Take short breaks between tasks	Get 8 hours of sleep	Drink enough water	Batch smaller tasks	Find your peak productivity time
Learn to say no	Set boundaries	Be realistic about your goals	Be intentional with your thoughts	Work smarter

You got this!

MONTHLY *planner*

Month: **Main focus:**

Week 1

Week 2

To-do list

- _____ ☐
- _____ ☐
- _____ ☐
- _____ ☐
- _____ ☐
- _____ ☐
- _____ ☐
- _____ ☐
- _____ ☐
- _____ ☐
- _____ ☐
- _____ ☐
- _____ ☐
- _____ ☐

Week 1

Week 2

Notes

WEEKLY *planner*

Week: **Quote:**

Monday

Tuesday

Wednesday

Thursday

Friday

Saturday

Sunday

WEEKLY *planner*

Week: **Quote:**

Monday

Tuesday

Wednesday

Thursday

Friday

Saturday

Sunday

WEEKLY *planner*

Week: **Quote:**

Monday

Tuesday

Wednesday

Thursday

Friday

Saturday

Sunday

WEEKLY *planner*

Week: **Quote:**

Monday

Tuesday

Wednesday

Thursday

Friday

Saturday

Sunday

FOCUS *planner*

Date -

Main focus -

Start date -

End date -

Breakdown of main focus

Smaller tasks to accomplish

☐
☐
☐
☐
☐
☐
☐
☐
☐
☐
☐

Notes

PROJECT *planner*

Start date

End date

Objective of project

MILESTONES

Task	Assigned to	Done

notes

TO-DO *list*

Date -

HIGH PRIORITY

○ _____
○ _____
○ _____
○ _____
○ _____
○ _____
○ _____
○ _____
○ _____
○ _____

LOW PRIORITY

○ _____
○ _____
○ _____
○ _____
○ _____
○ _____
○ _____
○ _____
○ _____
○ _____

Notes

_____
_____
_____

THINGS I *need to do*

Month - _____

Week _____

MONDAY
- [ ] _____
- [ ] _____
- [ ] _____
- [ ] _____
- [ ] _____

TUESDAY
- [ ] _____
- [ ] _____
- [ ] _____
- [ ] _____
- [ ] _____

WEDNESDAY
- [ ] _____
- [ ] _____
- [ ] _____
- [ ] _____
- [ ] _____

THURSDAY
- [ ] _____
- [ ] _____
- [ ] _____
- [ ] _____
- [ ] _____

FRIDAY
- [ ] _____
- [ ] _____
- [ ] _____
- [ ] _____
- [ ] _____

SATURDAY
- [ ] _____
- [ ] _____
- [ ] _____
- [ ] _____
- [ ] _____

SUNDAY
- [ ] _____
- [ ] _____
- [ ] _____
- [ ] _____
- [ ] _____

IMPORTANT NOTES
_____
_____
_____
_____
_____

MEETING *notes*

Meeting name/topic	Time	Date

Attendess

_____   _____
_____   _____
_____   _____
_____   _____

Agenda

_____
_____
_____
_____
_____
_____
_____

objectives

PRIORITY *matrix*

INSTRUCTIONS
List all the tasks you need to get done in the priority matrix below. Start with the most important and most urgent. The priority matrix will help you determine what needs to get done now and how you can better balance all the tasks that you need to do

	DO NOW	DO LATER
IMPORTANT	**GET IT DONE** (Important & urgent)	**SCHEDULE IT** (Important - not urgent)
NOT IMPORTANT	**DELEGATE IT** (Who else can do it)	**ELIMINATE IT** (not important, not urgent - delete)

BUCKET *list*

I BELIEVE IN MYSELF AND MY ABILITY TO SUCCEED.

AUGUST

MONDAY	TUESDAY	WEDNESDAY	THURSDAY	FRIDAY	SATURDAY	SUNDAY
☐	☐	☐	☐	☐	☐	☐
☐	☐	☐	☐	☐	☐	☐
☐	☐	☐	☐	☐	☐	☐
☐	☐	☐	☐	☐	☐	☐
☐	☐	☐	☐	☐	☐	☐
☐	☐	☐	☐	☐	☐	☐

30-DAY *productivity challenge*

30-days to becoming more productive!

Create a master to-do list	Take a 24 hour tv break	Take a break from social media	Do some goal planning	Work towards 1 goal today
Do 20 minutes of exercise	Clean your bedroom cupboards	Clean your kitchen cupboards	Wake up earlier	Reduce any distractions
Meet a new milestone	Organize your desktop	Plan your days in advance	Do meal planning	Create a productivity music playlist
Check your emails regularly	Do the most important thing first	Delegate an unimportant task	Make use of planning tools	Stop multitasking
Take short breaks between tasks	Get 8 hours of sleep	Drink enough water	Batch smaller tasks	Find your peak productivity time
Learn to say no	Set boundaries	Be realistic about your goals	Be intentional with your thoughts	Work *smarter*

You got this!

MONTHLY *planner*

Month: **Main focus:**

Week 1	Week 2

Week 1	Week 2

To-do list

- _____ ☐
- _____ ☐
- _____ ☐
- _____ ☐
- _____ ☐
- _____ ☐
- _____ ☐
- _____ ☐
- _____ ☐
- _____ ☐
- _____ ☐
- _____ ☐
- _____ ☐
- _____ ☐

Notes

WEEKLY *planner*

Week: **Quote:**

Monday

Tuesday

Wednesday

Thursday

Friday

Saturday

Sunday

WEEKLY *planner*

Week: **Quote:**

Monday

Tuesday

Wednesday

Thursday

Friday

Saturday

Sunday

WEEKLY *planner*

Week: **Quote:**

Monday

Tuesday

Wednesday

Thursday

Friday

Saturday

Sunday

WEEKLY *planner*

Week: **Quote:**

Monday

Tuesday

Wednesday

Thursday

Friday

Saturday

Sunday

FOCUS *planner*

Date -

Main focus -

Start date -

End date -

Breakdown of main focus

Smaller tasks to accomplish

- [ ]
- [ ]
- [ ]
- [ ]
- [ ]
- [ ]
- [ ]
- [ ]
- [ ]
- [ ]
- [ ]
- [ ]

Notes

PROJECT *planner*

Start date

End date

Objective of project

MILESTONES

Task	Assigned to	Done

notes

TO-DO *list*

Date -

HIGH PRIORITY | LOW PRIORITY

- ○ _____
- ○ _____
- ○ _____
- ○ _____
- ○ _____
- ○ _____
- ○ _____
- ○ _____
- ○ _____
- ○ _____

THINGS I *need to do*

Month -
_____

Week
_____

MONDAY
- [ ] _____
- [ ] _____
- [ ] _____
- [ ] _____
- [ ] _____

TUESDAY
- [ ] _____
- [ ] _____
- [ ] _____
- [ ] _____
- [ ] _____

WEDNESDAY
- [ ] _____
- [ ] _____
- [ ] _____
- [ ] _____
- [ ] _____

THURSDAY
- [ ] _____
- [ ] _____
- [ ] _____
- [ ] _____
- [ ] _____

FRIDAY
- [ ] _____
- [ ] _____
- [ ] _____
- [ ] _____
- [ ] _____

SATURDAY
- [ ] _____
- [ ] _____
- [ ] _____
- [ ] _____
- [ ] _____

SUNDAY
- [ ] _____
- [ ] _____
- [ ] _____
- [ ] _____
- [ ] _____

IMPORTANT NOTES
_____
_____
_____
_____
_____

MEETING *notes*

Meeting name/topic	Time	Date

Attendess

_____   _____
_____   _____
_____   _____
_____   _____

Agenda

_____
_____
_____
_____
_____
_____
_____

objectives

PRIORITY *matrix*

INSTRUCTIONS
List all the tasks you need to get done in the priority matrix below. Start with the most important and most urgent. The priority matrix will help you determine what needs to get done now and how you can better balance all the tasks that you need to do

	DO NOW	DO LATER
IMPORTANT	**GET IT DONE** (Important & urgent)	**SCHEDULE IT** (Important - not urgent)
NOT IMPORTANT	**DELEGATE IT** (Who else can do it)	**ELIMINATE IT** (not important, not urgent - delete)

BUCKET *list*

I WAS BORN WORTHY AND ENOUGH TO FOLLOW MY DREAMS CONFIDENTLY AND COURAGEOUSLY

SEPTEMBER

MONDAY	TUESDAY	WEDNESDAY	THURSDAY	FRIDAY	SATURDAY	SUNDAY
☐	☐	☐	☐	☐	☐	☐
☐	☐	☐	☐	☐	☐	☐
☐	☐	☐	☐	☐	☐	☐
☐	☐	☐	☐	☐	☐	☐
☐	☐	☐	☐	☐	☐	☐
☐	☐	☐	☐	☐	☐	☐

30-DAY *productivity challenge*

30-days to becoming more productive!

Create a master to-do list	Take a 24 hour tv break	Take a break from social media	Do some goal planning	Work towards 1 goal today
Do 20 minutes of exercise	Clean your bedroom cupboards	Clean your kitchen cupboards	Wake up earlier	Reduce any distractions
Meet a new milestone	Organize your desktop	Plan your days in advance	Do meal planning	Create a productivity music playlist
Check your emails regularly	Do the most important thing first	Delegate an unimportant task	Make use of planning tools	Stop multitasking
Take short breaks between tasks	Get 8 hours of sleep	Drink enough water	Batch smaller tasks	Find your peak productivity time
Learn to say no	Set boundaries	Be realistic about your goals	Be intentional with your thoughts	Work smarter

You got this!

MONTHLY *planner*

Month: **Main focus:**

Week 1	Week 2

To-do list

- _____ ☐
- _____ ☐
- _____ ☐
- _____ ☐
- _____ ☐
- _____ ☐
- _____ ☐
- _____ ☐
- _____ ☐
- _____ ☐
- _____ ☐
- _____ ☐
- _____ ☐
- _____ ☐

Week 1	Week 2

Notes

WEEKLY *planner*

Week: **Quote:**

Monday

Tuesday

Wednesday

Thursday

Friday

Saturday

Sunday

MONTHLY *planner*

Month: **Main focus:**

| Week 1 | Week 2 | To-do list |

| Week 1 | Week 2 |

Notes

WEEKLY *planner*

Week: **Quote:**

Monday

Tuesday

Wednesday

Thursday

Friday

Saturday

Sunday

WEEKLY *planner*

Week: **Quote:**

Monday

Tuesday

Wednesday

Thursday

Friday

Saturday

Sunday

WEEKLY planner

Week: _____   **Quote:**

Monday

Tuesday

Wednesday

Thursday

Friday

Saturday

Sunday

WEEKLY *planner*

Week: **Quote:**

Monday

Tuesday

Wednesday

Thursday

Friday

Saturday

Sunday

FOCUS *planner*

Date -

Main focus -

Start date -

End date -

Breakdown of main focus

Smaller tasks to accomplish

- [ ]
- [ ]
- [ ]
- [ ]
- [ ]
- [ ]
- [ ]
- [ ]
- [ ]
- [ ]
- [ ]

Notes

PROJECT *planner*

Start date

End date

Objective of project

MILESTONES

Task	Assigned to	Done

notes

TO-DO *list*

Date -

HIGH PRIORITY

○ _____
○ _____
○ _____
○ _____
○ _____
○ _____
○ _____
○ _____
○ _____
○ _____

LOW PRIORITY

○ _____
○ _____
○ _____
○ _____
○ _____
○ _____
○ _____
○ _____
○ _____
○ _____

Notes

_____
_____
_____

THINGS I *need to do*

Month - _____

Week _____

> " "

MONDAY
- [ ] _____
- [ ] _____
- [ ] _____
- [ ] _____
- [ ] _____

TUESDAY
- [ ] _____
- [ ] _____
- [ ] _____
- [ ] _____
- [ ] _____

WEDNESDAY
- [ ] _____
- [ ] _____
- [ ] _____
- [ ] _____
- [ ] _____

THURSDAY
- [ ] _____
- [ ] _____
- [ ] _____
- [ ] _____
- [ ] _____

FRIDAY
- [ ] _____
- [ ] _____
- [ ] _____
- [ ] _____
- [ ] _____

SATURDAY
- [ ] _____
- [ ] _____
- [ ] _____
- [ ] _____
- [ ] _____

SUNDAY
- [ ] _____
- [ ] _____
- [ ] _____
- [ ] _____
- [ ] _____

IMPORTANT NOTES
_____
_____
_____
_____
_____

MEETING *notes*

Meeting name/topic	Time	Date

Attendess

Agenda

objectives

PRIORITY *matrix*

INSTRUCTIONS
List all the tasks you need to get done in the priority matrix below. Start with the most important and most urgent. The priority matrix will help you determine what needs to get done now and how you can better balance all the tasks that you need to do

	DO NOW	DO LATER
IMPORTANT	**GET IT DONE** (Important & urgent)	**SCHEDULE IT** (Important - not urgent)
NOT IMPORTANT	**DELEGATE IT** (Who else can do it)	**ELIMINATE IT** (not important, not urgent - delete)

BUCKET *list*

○ _____ ○ _____
○ _____ ○ _____
○ _____ ○ _____
○ _____ ○ _____
○ _____ ○ _____
○ _____ ○ _____
○ _____ ○ _____
○ _____ ○ _____
○ _____ ○ _____
○ _____ ○ _____
○ _____ ○ _____
○ _____ ○ _____
○ _____ ○ _____
○ _____ ○ _____

I FOCUS ON BUILDING INCREDIBLE RELATIONSHIPS WITH MY COMMUNITY.

OCTOBER

MONDAY	TUESDAY	WEDNESDAY	THURSDAY	FRIDAY	SATURDAY	SUNDAY
☐	☐	☐	☐	☐	☐	☐
☐	☐	☐	☐	☐	☐	☐
☐	☐	☐	☐	☐	☐	☐
☐	☐	☐	☐	☐	☐	☐
☐	☐	☐	☐	☐	☐	☐
☐	☐	☐	☐	☐	☐	☐

30-DAY *productivity challenge*

30-days to becoming more productive!

Create a master to-do list	Take a 24 hour tv break	Take a break from social media	Do some goal planning	Work towards 1 goal today
Do 20 minutes of exercise	Clean your bedroom cupboards	Clean your kitchen cupboards	Wake up earlier	Reduce any distractions
Meet a new milestone	Organize your desktop	Plan your days in advance	Do meal planning	Create a productivity music playlist
Check your emails regularly	Do the most important thing first	Delegate an unimportant task	Make use of planning tools	Stop multitasking
Take short breaks between tasks	Get 8 hours of sleep	Drink enough water	Batch smaller tasks	Find your peak productivity time
Learn to say no	Set boundaries	Be realistic about your goals	Be intentional with your thoughts	Work smarter

You got this!

MONTHLY *planner*

Month: **Main focus:**

Week 1	Week 2
Week 1	Week 2

To-do list

- [ ] _____
- [ ] _____
- [ ] _____
- [ ] _____
- [ ] _____
- [ ] _____
- [ ] _____
- [ ] _____
- [ ] _____
- [ ] _____
- [ ] _____
- [ ] _____
- [ ] _____
- [ ] _____

Notes

WEEKLY *planner*

Week: **Quote:**

Monday

Tuesday

Wednesday

Thursday

Friday

Saturday

Sunday

WEEKLY *planner*

Week: **Quote:**

Monday

Tuesday

Wednesday

Thursday

Friday

Saturday

Sunday

WEEKLY *planner*

Week: **Quote:**

Monday

Tuesday

Wednesday

Thursday

Friday

Saturday

Sunday

WEEKLY *planner*

Week: **Quote:**

Monday

Tuesday

Wednesday

Thursday

Friday

Saturday

Sunday

FOCUS *planner*

Date -

Main focus -

Start date -

End date -

Breakdown of main focus

Smaller tasks to accomplish

- [ ]
- [ ]
- [ ]
- [ ]
- [ ]
- [ ]
- [ ]
- [ ]
- [ ]
- [ ]
- [ ]

Notes

PROJECT *planner*

Start date

End date

Objective of project

MILESTONES

Task	Assigned to	Done

notes

TO-DO list

Date -

HIGH PRIORITY | LOW PRIORITY

- ○ _____
- ○ _____
- ○ _____
- ○ _____
- ○ _____
- ○ _____
- ○ _____
- ○ _____
- ○ _____
- ○ _____

THINGS I *need to do*

Month -
_____

Week
_____

MONDAY
- [ ] _____
- [ ] _____
- [ ] _____
- [ ] _____
- [ ] _____

TUESDAY
- [ ] _____
- [ ] _____
- [ ] _____
- [ ] _____
- [ ] _____

WEDNESDAY
- [ ] _____
- [ ] _____
- [ ] _____
- [ ] _____
- [ ] _____

THURSDAY
- [ ] _____
- [ ] _____
- [ ] _____
- [ ] _____
- [ ] _____

FRIDAY
- [ ] _____
- [ ] _____
- [ ] _____
- [ ] _____
- [ ] _____

SATURDAY
- [ ] _____
- [ ] _____
- [ ] _____
- [ ] _____
- [ ] _____

SUNDAY
- [ ] _____
- [ ] _____
- [ ] _____
- [ ] _____
- [ ] _____

IMPORTANT NOTES
_____
_____
_____
_____
_____

MEETING *notes*

Meeting name/topic	Time	Date

Attendess

_____   _____
_____   _____
_____   _____
_____   _____

Agenda

_____
_____
_____
_____
_____
_____
_____

objectives

PRIORITY matrix

INSTRUCTIONS
List all the tasks you need to get done in the priority matrix below. Start with the most important and most urgent. The priority matrix will help you determine what needs to get done now and how you can better balance all the tasks that you need to do

	DO NOW	DO LATER
IMPORTANT	**GET IT DONE** (Important & urgent)	**SCHEDULE IT** (Important - not urgent)
NOT IMPORTANT	**DELEGATE IT** (Who else can do it)	**ELIMINATE IT** (not important, not urgent - delete)

BUCKET *list*

- ○ _____
- ○ _____
- ○ _____
- ○ _____
- ○ _____
- ○ _____
- ○ _____
- ○ _____
- ○ _____
- ○ _____
- ○ _____
- ○ _____
- ○ _____
- ○ _____

- ○ _____
- ○ _____
- ○ _____
- ○ _____
- ○ _____
- ○ _____
- ○ _____
- ○ _____
- ○ _____
- ○ _____
- ○ _____
- ○ _____
- ○ _____
- ○ _____

I ELEVATE TO NEW HEIGHTS OF ABUNDANCE AND SUCCESS EVERY MONTH.

NOVEMBER

MONDAY	TUESDAY	WEDNESDAY	THURSDAY	FRIDAY	SATURDAY	SUNDAY
☐	☐	☐	☐	☐	☐	☐
☐	☐	☐	☐	☐	☐	☐
☐	☐	☐	☐	☐	☐	☐
☐	☐	☐	☐	☐	☐	☐
☐	☐	☐	☐	☐	☐	☐
☐	☐	☐	☐	☐	☐	☐

30-DAY *productivity challenge*

30-days to becoming more productive!

Create a master to-do list	Take a 24 hour tv break	Take a break from social media	Do some goal planning	Work towards 1 goal today
Do 20 minutes of exercise	Clean your bedroom cupboards	Clean your kitchen cupboards	Wake up earlier	Reduce any distractions
Meet a new milestone	Organize your desktop	Plan your days in advance	Do meal planning	Create a productivity music playlist
Check your emails regularly	Do the most important thing first	Delegate an unimportant task	Make use of planning tools	Stop multitasking
Take short breaks between tasks	Get 8 hours of sleep	Drink enough water	Batch smaller tasks	Find your peak productivity time
Learn to say no	Set boundaries	Be realistic about your goals	Be intentional with your thoughts	Work smarter

You got this!

MONTHLY *planner*

Month: **Main focus:**

| Week 1 | Week 2 | To-do list |

- _____ ☐
- _____ ☐
- _____ ☐
- _____ ☐
- _____ ☐
- _____ ☐
- _____ ☐

| Week 1 | Week 2 |

- _____ ☐
- _____ ☐
- _____ ☐
- _____ ☐
- _____ ☐
- _____ ☐
- _____ ☐

Notes

WEEKLY *planner*

Week: **Quote:**

Monday

Tuesday

Wednesday

Thursday

Friday

Saturday

Sunday

WEEKLY *planner*

Week: **Quote:**

Monday

Tuesday

Wednesday

Thursday

Friday

Saturday

Sunday

WEEKLY *planner*

Week: **Quote:**

Monday

Tuesday

Wednesday

Thursday

Friday

Saturday

Sunday

WEEKLY *planner*

Week: **Quote:**

Monday

Tuesday

Wednesday

Thursday

Friday

Saturday

Sunday

FOCUS *planner*

Date -

Main focus -

Start date -

End date -

Breakdown of main focus

Smaller tasks to accomplish

- [ ]
- [ ]
- [ ]
- [ ]
- [ ]
- [ ]
- [ ]
- [ ]
- [ ]
- [ ]
- [ ]

Notes

PROJECT *planner*

Start date

End date

Objective of project

MILESTONES

Task	Assigned to	Done

notes

TO-DO *list*

Date -

HIGH PRIORITY | LOW PRIORITY

○ _____ ○ _____
○ _____ ○ _____
○ _____ ○ _____
○ _____ ○ _____
○ _____ ○ _____
○ _____ ○ _____
○ _____ ○ _____
○ _____ ○ _____
○ _____ ○ _____
○ _____ ○ _____

Notes

_____
_____
_____

THINGS I *need to do*

Month - _____

Week _____

MONDAY
- _____ ☐
- _____ ☐
- _____ ☐
- _____ ☐
- _____ ☐

TUESDAY
- _____ ☐
- _____ ☐
- _____ ☐
- _____ ☐
- _____ ☐

WEDNESDAY
- _____ ☐
- _____ ☐
- _____ ☐
- _____ ☐
- _____ ☐

THURSDAY
- _____ ☐
- _____ ☐
- _____ ☐
- _____ ☐
- _____ ☐

FRIDAY
- _____ ☐
- _____ ☐
- _____ ☐
- _____ ☐
- _____ ☐

SATURDAY
- _____ ☐
- _____ ☐
- _____ ☐
- _____ ☐
- _____ ☐

SUNDAY
- _____ ☐
- _____ ☐
- _____ ☐
- _____ ☐
- _____ ☐

IMPORTANT NOTES
_____
_____
_____
_____
_____

MEETING *notes*

Meeting name/topic	Time	Date

Attendess

---------------------------   ---------------------------
---------------------------   ---------------------------
---------------------------   ---------------------------
---------------------------   ---------------------------

Agenda

---

objectives

PRIORITY *matrix*

INSTRUCTIONS
List all the tasks you need to get done in the priority matrix below. Start with the most important and most urgent. The priority matrix will help you determine what needs to get done now and how you can better balance all the tasks that you need to do

	DO NOW	DO LATER
IMPORTANT	**GET IT DONE** (Important & urgent)	**SCHEDULE IT** (Important - not urgent)
NOT IMPORTANT	**DELEGATE IT** (Who else can do it)	**ELIMINATE IT** (not important, not urgent - delete)

BUCKET list

MY DREAM CLIENTS ALWAYS SHOW UP EASILY AND EFFORTLESSLY.

DECEMBER

MONDAY	TUESDAY	WEDNESDAY	THURSDAY	FRIDAY	SATURDAY	SUNDAY
☐	☐	☐	☐	☐	☐	☐
☐	☐	☐	☐	☐	☐	☐
☐	☐	☐	☐	☐	☐	☐
☐	☐	☐	☐	☐	☐	☐
☐	☐	☐	☐	☐	☐	☐
☐	☐	☐	☐	☐	☐	☐

30-DAY productivity challenge

30-days to becoming more productive!

Create a master to-do list	Take a 24 hour tv break	Take a break from social media	Do some goal planning	Work towards 1 goal today
Do 20 minutes of exercise	Clean your bedroom cupboards	Clean your kitchen cupboards	Wake up earlier	Reduce any distractions
Meet a new milestone	Organize your desktop	Plan your days in advance	Do meal planning	Create a productivity music playlist
Check your emails regularly	Do the most important thing first	Delegate an unimportant task	Make use of planning tools	Stop multitasking
Take short breaks between tasks	Get 8 hours of sleep	Drink enough water	Batch smaller tasks	Find your peak productivity time
Learn to say no	Set boundaries	Be realistic about your goals	Be intentional with your thoughts	Work smarter

You got this!

MONTHLY *planner*

Month: _____ **Main focus:** _____

| Week 1 | Week 2 |

To-do list

_____ ☐
_____ ☐
_____ ☐
_____ ☐
_____ ☐
_____ ☐
_____ ☐
_____ ☐
_____ ☐
_____ ☐
_____ ☐
_____ ☐
_____ ☐
_____ ☐

| Week 1 | Week 2 |

Notes

WEEKLY *planner*

Week: **Quote:**

Monday

Tuesday

Wednesday

Thursday

Friday

Saturday

Sunday

WEEKLY *planner*

Week: **Quote:**

Monday

Tuesday

Wednesday

Thursday

Friday

Saturday

Sunday

WEEKLY *planner*

Week: **Quote:**

Monday

Tuesday

Wednesday

Thursday

Friday

Saturday

Sunday

WEEKLY *planner*

Week: **Quote:**

Monday

Tuesday

Wednesday

Thursday

Friday

Saturday

Sunday

FOCUS *planner*

Date -

Main focus -

Start date -

End date -

Breakdown of main focus

Smaller tasks to accomplish

- [ ]
- [ ]
- [ ]
- [ ]
- [ ]
- [ ]
- [ ]
- [ ]
- [ ]
- [ ]
- [ ]

Notes

TO-DO *list*

Date -

HIGH PRIORITY

○ _____
○ _____
○ _____
○ _____
○ _____
○ _____
○ _____
○ _____
○ _____
○ _____

LOW PRIORITY

○ _____
○ _____
○ _____
○ _____
○ _____
○ _____
○ _____
○ _____
○ _____
○ _____

Notes

_____
_____
_____

THINGS I *need to do*

Month - _____

Week _____

"   "

MONDAY
- _____ ☐
- _____ ☐
- _____ ☐
- _____ ☐
- _____ ☐

TUESDAY
- _____ ☐
- _____ ☐
- _____ ☐
- _____ ☐
- _____ ☐

WEDNESDAY
- _____ ☐
- _____ ☐
- _____ ☐
- _____ ☐
- _____ ☐

THURSDAY
- _____ ☐
- _____ ☐
- _____ ☐
- _____ ☐
- _____ ☐

FRIDAY
- _____ ☐
- _____ ☐
- _____ ☐
- _____ ☐
- _____ ☐

SATURDAY
- _____ ☐
- _____ ☐
- _____ ☐
- _____ ☐
- _____ ☐

SUNDAY
- _____ ☐
- _____ ☐
- _____ ☐
- _____ ☐
- _____ ☐

IMPORTANT NOTES
_____
_____
_____
_____
_____

MEETING *notes*

Meeting name/topic	Time	Date

Attendess

Agenda

objectives

PRIORITY matrix

INSTRUCTIONS
List all the tasks you need to get done in the priority matrix below. Start with the most important and most urgent. The priority matrix will help you determine what needs to get done now and how you can better balance all the tasks that you need to do

	DO NOW	DO LATER
IMPORTANT	**GET IT DONE** (Important & urgent)	**SCHEDULE IT** (Important - not urgent)
NOT IMPORTANT	**DELEGATE IT** (Who else can do it)	**ELIMINATE IT** (not important, not urgent - delete)

BUCKET *list*

- ○ _____
- ○ _____
- ○ _____
- ○ _____
- ○ _____
- ○ _____
- ○ _____
- ○ _____
- ○ _____
- ○ _____
- ○ _____
- ○ _____
- ○ _____
- ○ _____
- ○ _____

- ○ _____
- ○ _____
- ○ _____
- ○ _____
- ○ _____
- ○ _____
- ○ _____
- ○ _____
- ○ _____
- ○ _____
- ○ _____
- ○ _____
- ○ _____
- ○ _____

PROJECT *planner*

Start date

End date

Objective of project

MILESTONES

Task	Assigned to	Done

notes

GOAL
planning
and tracking

S.M.A.R.T goals

INSTRUCTIONS
Specific - Identify a specific goal that is detail orientated
Measurable - How will you measure or track the goal you're working towards
Attainable - What actions, skills, and resources will help you achieve the goal
Relevant - How does this goal align with your long-term goals and aspirations
Time-orientated - What is the time frame that you want to complete this goal by

Specific

Measurable

Attainable

Relevant

Time-orientated

ANNUAL goals

INSTRUCTIONS
Write down the biggest goals you have for the next 12 months. Make at least 2 of them a skill. Learning new skills will make you feel empowered, confident, and accomplished in your business. Write down your WHY to make sure this goal connects with you and then set a realistic deadline.

THE GOAL	WHY	WHEN

THE GOAL	WHY	WHEN

THE GOAL	WHY	WHEN

QUARTERLY *goals*

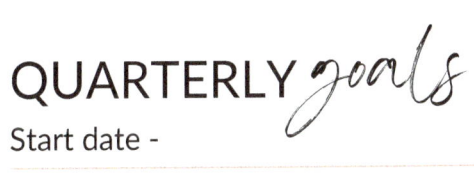

Start date -   End date -

	THE BIG GOAL	ACTION STEPS
QUARTER 1		• • • •

Start date -   End date -

	THE BIG GOAL	ACTION STEPS
QUARTER 2		• • • •

Start date -   End date -

	THE BIG GOAL	ACTION STEPS
QUARTER 3		• • • •

Start date -   End date -

	THE BIG GOAL	ACTION STEPS
QUARTER 4		• • • •

GOAL breakdown

The big goal -

Broken into small steps

- [ ] _____
- [ ] _____
- [ ] _____
- [ ] _____

- [ ] _____
- [ ] _____
- [ ] _____
- [ ] _____

The big goal -

Broken into small steps

- [ ] _____
- [ ] _____
- [ ] _____
- [ ] _____

- [ ] _____
- [ ] _____
- [ ] _____
- [ ] _____

The big goal -

Broken into small steps

- [ ] _____
- [ ] _____
- [ ] _____
- [ ] _____

- [ ] _____
- [ ] _____
- [ ] _____
- [ ] _____

The big goal -

Broken into small steps

- [ ] _____
- [ ] _____
- [ ] _____
- [ ] _____

- [ ] _____
- [ ] _____
- [ ] _____
- [ ] _____

MY *goals*

	Goal	Action plan
3 MONTHS	_____	_____

	Goal	Action plan
6 MONTHS	_____	_____

	Goal	Action plan
1 YEAR	_____	_____

FINANCIAL
tracking
and planning

INCOME *goals*

Reflect on your income & expenses for the year.

Month	Income	Expenses	Profit	Comments
January				
February				
March				
April				
May				
June				
July				
August				
September				
October				
November				
December				
TOTAL				

What were the best & worst months and possible reasons why?

FINANCAL

Goal	Action Steps
Start	End
Progress	○○○○○○○○○○○○○○

Goal	Action Steps
Start	End
Progress	○○○○○○○○○○○○○○

Goal	Action Steps
Start	End
Progress	○○○○○○○○○○○○○○

PASSWORD *tracker*

Account/website	Username/email	Password

FINANCE *overview*

Year -

Month	Savings	Income	Expenses	Debt
January				
February				
March				
April				
May				
June				
July				
August				
September				
October				
November				
December				
Sub-total				

Note-taking

Note-taking

Note-taking